From Rough Draft to Published

A Beginner's Guide to Publishing

by Kathryn Fletcher

Printed in the United States of America

Library of Congress Cataloging-in-Publication data
Fletcher, Kathryn
From Rough Draft to Published: A Beginner's Guide to Publishing / Kathryn Fletcher
p.134
12.7 x 20.32 cm. (5 x 8 in)
ISBN: 978-1-7348847-0-8
Library of Congress Control Number: 2020907321
1. Non-Fiction— Authorship — Publication.
I. Fletcher, Kathryn.
II. From Rough Draft to Published: A Beginner's Guide to Publication. First Edition.

Publisher: Quill & Books
Editor: Beverly J. Mardis (bjmardiseditor@yahoo.com)
Copy Editor: Dianne McBride
Cover Design: Bobby Birchall of Bobby & Co.

For Jesse and Levi

Table of Contents

Note from the Author

Why am I writing this?

Last year when one of my short stories was published, several students sought me out and asked me how to get published. What are all the steps from rough draft to published? I thought about all the lessons I've learned over the years which I could share.

I told them a little about the process, but there was so much that I couldn't really sum it up in a 10 minute conversation. I felt like I should be able to recommend a book to read, because that's what I do. (I'm a librarian at my core.) I could recommend a dozen different books on writing, but when talking to students, I'm not sure that would be very encouraging because it would be so overwhelming. I didn't know of many books about publishing; most of what I've learned about publishing comes from talking to editors and others who work in the publishing industry.

My students wanted to know how to find

publishers, how to submit their writing, what does an agent do, and more. Those are things I can share in a small book that is short and to the point, giving the basics. The purpose of this book is to let beginning writers know a little bit about the world of publication and the steps between writing a rough draft and publishing a short story or novel. I will say though, every person's path to publication is different. This information is based on my path and what I've learned through reading thousands of words in books and blogs, listening to countless hours of podcasts, and going to writing conferences. The information comes from published authors, editors, agents, and from my own experience.

Who is this book for?

A serious writer. Someone that wants to make writing novels your career or maybe a side hustle until you get enough books published to make it a career. You might be a teenager and want to get an early start. Is it possible? Yes! There are a number of teens whose work has been published before they turned twenty. Is reading this book going to guarantee success? No. Could it help you navigate this path a bit easier? Yes.

Or you might be a person like me, who at age 39 realized I always dreamed of being a writer and time was slipping away. So I thought, "I better get started now."

Why do you need this book?

If you skip steps between writing the rough draft and submitting it to your dream publisher, you will almost certainly have your manuscript rejected, and you only get *one* chance with that publisher for that manuscript. So this book can help you get published because you won't be ignorant of the process.

People often imagine authors like J.K. Rowling sat down, wrote a manuscript, sent it off to a publisher, and voila! She was suddenly a millionaire. No. She toiled over that manuscript for 7 years. J.K. Rowling's manuscript was actually rejected by 12 publishers before Bloomsbury picked it up. There is much that the general public doesn't normally hear about the publication process.

Getting a traditional publishing deal is not easy, but self-publishing has its own challenges. The rewards of getting your story out into the world are exciting and well worth the effort. Likely you know that traditional publishing is not the only route anymore, and self-publishing doesn't have the stigma it once did. I'll give you pros and cons about both paths so you can make an informed decision that is right for you.

Part 1

Rough Draft

Chapter 1

Writer Types

To Begin

You've always dreamed of becoming published. You are a person of action, so you sit down and write a novel, a poem, a short story, a memoir, or whatever you feel compelled to write.

For the rough draft, concentrate on getting your ideas down on the page. Do not worry about your audience, getting published, or what your friends will think. Just get everything down on paper for now.

Try different methods of writing and different exercises. See what works for you and what doesn't. There is no right or wrong way of getting the rough draft done.

Discovery Writer or Outliner?

When meeting other writers they will often ask you if you are a discovery writer or an outliner. What's the difference between the two? There are many terms for these two types of writers: discovery writer, pantser, plotter, and outliner. (To name a few)

What are they?

What kind of writer are you?

Is one better than the other?

Some will say yes and get rather snobby about it. Ignore them. Neither is better or worse—just different.

What is a Discovery Writer?

Discovery writers may also be called pantsers because they write by the seat of their pants. These writers tend to have an idea for a character or a situation, so they sit down and start writing. They write to discover what the character has to say. They write to discover what would happen given a certain situation. They write to explore ideas and life.

Sometimes they will do some pre-planning, not an outline, but a character interview perhaps. They sit down and start writing as if they are interviewing their character to learn who that person is and what they are like. Other times they will take the POV (point of view) of the character and put them in a situation to see how they react. This is not meant to be part of the story, just a way for the writer to get to know the character. This is how they can discover that character's voice, attitude, and motivations. Once they have this, they can begin writing the story in earnest.

What is an Outliner?

Outliners can also be called plotters because they plot much of the story out before they begin writing. These writers have an idea for a character or a situation, so they sit down and make an outline. They may do a character sketch. They may use a specific formula to organize their thoughts, or they might not. They do a lot of planning before they write the first scene. They often love spreadsheets and use them to organize magic systems, government organization, political structures, and other world-building elements.

There are many different outlining methods they can use. One of the most popular is the 3 Act Structure. It started out as a structure for movies, but has been adapted for books.

Dan Wells has a lecture on his 7 Point Story Structure. This is the one that I like best and use as a loose guide for my fiction short stories and novels.

I used the Dan Wells structure in the way that he describes in the videos. It helped me get a feel for writing with structure. Now, after writing dozens of stories, I have a feel for it, so I don't plot stories with the form I created but I have it in the back of my mind as I develop the outline.

One of the most famous structures is called the Hero's Journey. A man named Joseph Campbell studied myths across all the cultures he could. He looked at stories that had endured for centuries and looked for commonalities. What came of that research was a book called The Hero with a Thousand Faces. He put together those commonalities into a story structure called The Hero's Journey. You will hear people reference these stages when they talk about story structure so it is good to get familiar with them.

1. The Ordinary World
2. The Call of Adventure
3. Refusal of the Call
4. Meeting the Mentor
5. Crossing the First Threshold
6. Tests, Allies, Enemies
7. Approach to the Inmost Cave
8. The Ordeal
9. Reward
10. The Road Back
11. Resurrection
12. Return with the Elixir

Some authors use these structures *after* they write the story or outline. They use it as a tool to diagnose what is wrong, when something with the story is broken, rather than as a map to write the story.

Which one are you?

The way people categorize authors as one or the other makes you think there are two boxes and you fit into one or the other. The truth is, very few or possibly nobody is exclusively one or the other. We all fall on a spectrum that leans one way or another.

On the Writing Excuses podcast, they tease Brandon Sanderson about being a crazy-outliner. He has outlines of his outlines they say...which means he even outlines his scenes. He churns out a massive amount of published words each year and his books are successful, so, hey, it works for him.

At the opposite end of the spectrum is Stephen King. He is a pantser. This is what he says about discovery writing:

> "Stories are relics, part of an undiscovered pre-existing world. The writer's job is to use the tools in his or her toolbox to get as much of each one out of the ground intact as possible. Sometimes the fossil you uncover is small; a seashell. Sometimes it's enormous; a Tyrannosaurus Rex with all those gigantic ribs and grinning teeth. Either way, a short story or thousand-page whopper of a novel, the techniques of excavation remain the same."
>
> -Stephen King, *On Writing*

He also produces a massive amount of published words each year and to say his books are successful is an understatement.

Some outliners may have the major plot points planned out, but they discovery write when they connect the dots.

Often discovery writers don't have an outline written down, but in their head, they have certain events that they know are going to happen somewhere along the way.

When I was a pantser, I had the major plot points or a general direction in my head. I even had some smaller events planned for the next couple chapters in my head, even as I wrote the chapters.

So really it is a matter of where on the spectrum you fall. Try out both ways and find out which feels right for you. Regardless of where you are on the spectrum, don't force yourself to be what you are not; that is how creativity is killed!

Advantages and Disadvantages

There are advantages and disadvantages to both methods of writing. Many new writers begin as discovery writers. One disadvantage to discovery writing is that it is sometimes circuitous. You may write a few thousand words which will later need to be cut from the story because they were irrelevant. As King says, it is like archeology. A ton of earth must be dug through before you get to the goal of your dig. Discovery writers put a ton of words on the page.

Most writers have notebooks to collect words, phrases, snippets of ideas. Both discovery writers and outliners have some kind of computer folder in which they collect words which had to be cut. I can't remember for sure who it was but I think it is Dan Wells that has named his folder "Graveyard" for story "bones" which he can't use now, but at some point may be able to resurrect or cannibalize for another story. (He writes excellent horror and science fiction stories!)

The advantage of discovery writing is that these writers are often in tune with their characters. They listen to them, so the characters behave naturally on the page.

Sometimes I'll discovery write a little bit to find out what the character's voice sounds like. Usually that text gets tossed, but it served its purpose, so it wasn't a waste.

Sometimes writers are more inclined to outline. I moved further down the spectrum towards outliner when I learned that discovery writers tend to throw out more words.

Much of the discovery for an outliner happens in their head rather than on the paper or computer screen.

The disadvantage to being an outliner is that sometimes the story becomes stilted. It becomes movement from plot point to plot point without the necessary heart. New outliners tend to stick too closely to the outline and are afraid to deviate when necessary.

As I said, I lean more toward being an outliner, but I still do some discovery writing. I discovery write to play with the tone of a story. For my most recent short story, I rewrote the first page three times before I finally felt like I got it right.

Try jotting down and planning a bunch of ideas before getting started on the first sentence of the story.

Brainstorm the magic system, the setting, the personalities of characters, the theme, the conflict, subplots, and the major plot points of the story before sentence number one. Discovery write individual scenes between the major plot points.

Sometimes characters lead me down a different path than I expect. If it is a better path, I will change my outline as needed. Usually though, my characters aren't such divas that demand major changes. Often, they are cleverer than me at connecting the dots between scenes.

Neither outliner nor discovery writer is right or wrong, better or worse than the other. They are both valid storytelling methods. Successful authors exist at both ends of the spectrum and everywhere between. It is important to try both methods to see where on the spectrum you feel most comfortable. Additionally, it is important to learn the pitfalls of each, so you can overcome the weaknesses within that method.

Further Reading on Planning

The Hero with a Thousand Faces by Joseph Campbell (Academic Level Reading!)

The Hero's Journey by Christopher Vogler

Dan Wells 7 Point Story Structure
https://www.youtube.com/watch?v=KcmiqQ9NpPE
https://www.youtube.com/watch?v=mrP9604BEOM
https://www.youtube.com/watch?v=NNZDL9-dN8k
https://www.youtube.com/watch?v=0WC_WWErNd8
https://www.youtube.com/watch?v=jD-T-ku4ynk

Three Act Structure
https://en.wikipedia.org/wiki/Three-act_structure

The Hero's Journey
https://blog.reedsy.com/heros-journey/ for a simpler breakdown of The Hero's Journey

My Planning Page
and all the above links are in the Writer's Resources Vault https://www.subscribepage.com/resource-vault

Chapter 2

Revisions and Edits

Self-Editing

Back in April 2017, I finished the really rough draft of my almost 100,000-word manuscript. I celebrated. I printed that monster out on paper. I didn't care that it used almost a whole ink cartridge and a whole ream of paper. I was so happy to have finished my first manuscript.

I knew it should rest for a bit before starting to edit. Frankly, I was happy about that. But months later, when I looked at it, knowing I needed to edit it. I shook my head. No. It was too big a task. Truthfully, I was well aware that the story was a *hot mess*. I had whole plot threads left dangling and snarled knots that you wouldn't believe! (And that is okay! First drafts are supposed to be that way.)

Not only is the manuscript a huge disaster, but

revisions require thinking about so much. How was I ever going to tackle all that?

I came up with a plan: do a few short stories and hone my editing skills on something smaller, more manageable, then go back to the hot mess. It was through those stories that I found a good revision process. It is still evolving and I think it always will be because I'm not one to ever stop trying to improve. Semper in Doctrina! (translated: Always learning!)

I began to learn the process by researching how the authors I admire do their revisions. Most will say to revise in passes. For example:

Pass 1. Plot
Pass 2. Character
Pass 3. World Building
Pass 4. Dialogue and Prose

Tackle each of these one-by-one to avoid running in endless circles. That is easier said than done, if you are as easily distracted as me. When I stumble upon a problem I usually want to fix it then and there. Trust me though: Keep a notebook next to your computer to jot down notes of things to fix later during the appropriate pass. By taking on one thing at a time, you can remain focused on that task and that is enough. Imagine this:

If I do a little plot fixing and discover an issue with a character's dialogue in this scene. I stop to fix the dialogue throughout the scene. In the next chapter, I discover a plot issue with not enough foreshadowing, but there is also an issue with the description of the library in this scene. It says there is green carpet but I think in chapter 4 it said blue carpet. I go back to chapter 4 and look it up, yep blue. Well which one should it be? I think in chapter 8 there is a description of a room that is green and I don't want all my rooms to look the same so this library carpet should be blue. Okay. That is solved. Now where was I? Chapter 7. I was working on plot stuff. Change the carpet color. I need to adjust what this character does in this scene to foreshadow the event in chapter 18, *right*?

Do you see how these little side trips into carpet color and other unrelated details can interrupt your flow when working on plot? Instead it could have been just a little note in the notebook: "Chapter 7: Library carpet color blue or green?" That kind of thing can wait until round 3 revisions of world building.

Once you have these areas of revision complete, then you can work on edits.

Which Comes First: Revisions or Edits?

I always do revisions first and edits as the very last thing. Some prefer to do both at the same time but it seems to create a lot of extra work for me.

This is what I teach my students. I didn't make it up, so the brilliance is not mine. I would cite my source but it is all over the internet. I don't know the original inventor.

Revisions are the A.R.M.S.

Add- Add information that was missing–Material that is important to the story.

Remove- Take out unnecessary information

Move- Move sentences or even scenes around for better effect.

Substitute- rewrite scenes that need it for whatever reason.

Edits are the C.U.P.S.

Capitalization

Usage

Punctuation

Spelling

I don't see the sense in looking at C.U.P.S. before I do revisions. I am highly likely to forget to capitalize stuff, forget commas, and mess up grammar when I am rearranging and rewriting scenes. So it makes sense to me to do revisions first. (I've seen others recommend edits first, but that doesn't work for me.)

Revision Passes

Are there big glaring problems? Reread the story as a reader would. Try to be objective. That is why we let it rest for a bit, to get some distance.

Look for plot holes, things you forgot to explain,

and basically any massive sweeping problems that need to be fixed.

Some people keep track of this *as* they write their rough draft so they don't forget to later fix problems. By writing them down, it frees them to move on with the rough draft. (I, however, am not yet this organized. I'm working on it though.)

Once you have this list of major problems from beginning to end, start working on them. Do not start working on them when you are halfway through the draft or you might fall into the downward spiral of write-revise-write-revise-write-revise. If you go through the whole document and view it holistically, it is better than a micro-view of the document.

Plot

Have you foreshadowed what needs to be foreshadowed? Is the foreshadowing enough or too much?

Is the conflict engaging enough?

Are the motivations reasonable?

Are the decisions plausible?

Is there a simpler solution that your character could take?

Pacing

Are there slow parts? You might need to move some scenes around to control the pacing. (Round 1 Beta readers are really good at helping you see this!)

Cuts also come into play here. Four pages of straight description will bring your pacing to a grinding halt. Break up large swaths of description with some action beats and break up large chunks of action with a sprinkling of description.

Here are some ways to affect the pacing of a story.
To quicken the pace you can:

- Shorten chapters, paragraphs, and/or sentence length
- Write dialogue to show the conversation instead of describing the conversation
- End the chapter on a cliffhanger or a reveal
- Take out backstory or flashbacks when possible
- Remove unnecessary subplots
- Add action scenes between slower scenes

To slow the pace you can:

- Lengthen chapters, paragraphs, and/or sentences
- Focus on and describe the details of a significant event, item, or person
- Add introspection (aka navel gazing) to further develop characters and their motivations
- Add flashbacks or backstory if needed

- Add a subplot if needed

Know the pacing expectations of your genre.

- Action is fast paced.
- Realistic fiction allows for a slower, more thoughtful pace.
- Thriller has the quickest pacing of all. Chapters need to end at a point where the reader can't put the book down.
- YA chapters should be shorter to give kids a sense of accomplishment and keep their attention. Even paragraphs should be kept short.

Character Development

Look at each character in your story. Did they turn out the way you hoped? Or did they take on a life of their own and go in a different direction? Is that working for you? Have you fleshed out the characters well? Do they all have goals of their own? Sometimes those goals are contradictory to the main plot which makes for some interesting plot twists and character dynamics.

Are there any Mary Sues? A Mary Sue is a character without flaws. They always say the right thing. They do the right thing. They are perfect. They are also unrealistic and unrelatable. You want your character to be human and that means they have flaws or weaknesses.

Perhaps your character suffers from self-doubt, anxiety, kleptomania, arrogance, talks too much, or maybe they are generous to a fault.

Look at each character carefully. Do the main characters have a complete arc? A character arc is the transformation of a character within the story or series.

Most modern stories are character–centered, which means the characters need to evolve. Quite often the main character starts off *wanting* one thing, when really they *need* something else. Over the course of the story, the main character learns what it is that he needs, and goes after that. K.M. Weiland has an excellent book and workbook to help you if you wish to read more on this topic.

Voice

Does the narrator's voice remain consistent throughout? How present is the narrator's voice. What effect do you want to have? Do you want an invisible narrator or would you rather a very present one? I love reading books like *The Girl Who Drank the Moon* by Kelly Barnhill. This book is written in 3rd person omniscient and reads like a person is telling you a fairy tale. Absolutely stunning storytelling! Perfect for this story, but that isn't the right narrator voice for all stories.

Does each character have their own voice or do all your characters sound the same?

Check dialogue. Is it realistic or stilted and fake? Is each character consistent in their tone? Does each character have a unique voice? Think about character backgrounds. A well-educated character will likely speak differently than an uneducated one.

Trim the Fat

I've heard different authors give different numbers but most go through and try to cut between 10-20% of their word count to tighten their writing. Apparently, we all, even the best authors, fall prey to overindulgence. Many science fiction & fantasy writers indulge in too much world-building and have to carefully control it.

Very new writers are particularly susceptible to purple prose. Purple prose is writing with far too much description that uses every single big word in your vocabulary.

Here is an example of purple prose that I wrote back in my 20s:

"John's bony, transparent hands clutched a walking stick. A wispy, white beard hung over his gaunt belly. John looked at his feet, the earth was sticky with blood. Such was the fate of the people of this land. The spattering of trees around him were twisted, gnarled and void of leaves except for a few crunchy brown ones hanging on. The air was dry and a scorching breeze swept the kingdom. At the horizon, the sun hung low, partly shrouded by rusty clouds. Onyx blue darkness crept up the opposite side of the sky."

Did you actually read all that? I doubt it. Look at

all the super fancy adjectives. Purple prose is a sign of insecurity, of trying too hard.

Tone down that purple prose. Remove non-essential scenes, paragraphs, sentences, characters and even words. Look at each scene, each sentence. Can it be cut? What purpose is it serving? If you are writing a short story, then you have to be ruthless. The writing must be tight. Longer works will allow a little more indulging, but not an endless supply.

Sometimes even characters must be removed from the story. Think about what purpose they serve. Are they there to toss out a joke here and there? Or are they acting as a foil for your protagonist? If it is just for the jokes, you can maybe give the jokes to another character and edit this one out, or find other ways to cut the tension when needed. Sometimes two characters can be combined as one.

Edits

After I've looked at all those items and fixed them, I go through and do an editing pass...or 5 billion passes.

This is when I look at:

- sentence structure
- comma placement
- run-ons
- fragments

19

- spellings
- punctuation

I might play with using semicolons or M dashes (those are long dashes). I adjust paragraphing for dramatic effect as needed. Spelling…oh spelling…the bane of my existence! Please use spell check but don't rely soul-ly on that! See what I did there? Don't rely solely on spellcheck. That program is not yet smart enough to help you with homophones. Plus these kinds of mistakes can make you seem amateurish. Also use Grammarly or a similar program, if you can, to help catch sentence structure mistakes. But just because you've run spell check and a grammar program on it, don't assume there are no mistakes left to be found. The English language is complex and the human brain is still smarter than a computer program…so far.

Do all this. Then you can look into having a professional editor look at your work.

Professional Editors and the Types of Edits

Developmental Edits

The kinds of things a developmental editor looks for are major story elements.

- Plot holes- a part of the story that is missing or the author missed an obvious solution to the conflict, a simpler one.

- Story Structure- Does your story follow a traditional structure or is it a wonky mess?
- Inconsistencies- Are Barbara's eyes green on page 4 but brown on page 44?
- Character development- Does each of your main characters complete their arc? Are the arcs plausible?
- Story arc - Does the story come to a natural and satisfying conclusion?

With my current novel, I wrote a 3 page synopsis of the whole novel I'm planning and gave it to my editor. She and I went over it and discussed the possibilities for how to fill in certain gaps I still had in the outline. I like doing this because it gives her an opportunity to punch any holes in the plot now when it is only 3 pages long, rather than after I have a hundred pages written. I can easily make adjustments to the synopsis.

If you are a discovery writer, this will not work. You can give your manuscript to a developmental editor after you've written it and make changes if needed from there.

The developmental editor looks at the story as a whole. This type of editor will offer suggestions for sweeping changes to the story that will make it stronger. They might say that the character motivation is too weak. That the villain behaves too predictably.

Most people bristle when they get negative feedback. We are human. Do not react at first though. Don't dismiss their advice out of hand. If you can't say anything positive, then don't say anything. Let the advice sink in for a day…a week…however much time you need to look back at it objectively. A good editor knows their business. Listen to them. Consider what they say. Humor them. Give their advice a try and see what happens. You might like what comes of it.

For example, my editor was working on a novel for a client. It had 20 POVs, all in first person. She suggested that it be changed to third person. Initially the client balked, but eventually gave it a try. After the client tried it they found that they liked it even better and saw the advantage.

It is not all bad though. They will also tell you the good in your story. They will tell you that your main character is entertaining. That the plot twist you created is brilliant.

A good editor will not try to hijack your story, they merely offer enhancements to your story to make it shine.

Line Edits & Copy Edits

There is a blurry line between these two types of editing. Some say they are synonyms while others say there is a difference. If there is a distinction, it is subtle. These editors go line by line through your manuscript looking for small mistakes such as grammar, punctuation, spelling, and style. They might also make adjustments to transitions and solve wordiness issues. These changes are all at the sentence level.

Proofreader

This person will also go through the manuscript line by line looking for typos and formatting errors. This is the very last step before pressing the print button at the printing press. This can be a professional you hire. It can also be a friend who finds joy in searching for mistakes. (Not a friend that is going to glance and say, "Yeah, sure looks good.")

When I was in middle school, a friend of mine used to watch black and white westerns searching for mistakes, such as one of the extras wearing a modern day wrist watch. This is the kind of person I need to proofread for me, if they are good at grammar.

Further Reading on Revision and Editing

Novel Revision Processes
http://www.tomiadeyemi.com/blog/the-best-way-to-revise-your-novel

https://www.thecreativepenn.com/2017/10/05/9-steps-revising-your-novel/

http://themanuscriptshredder.com/novel-revision-and-editing-guide/

https://www.annelyle.com/for-writers/10-step-novel-revision/

Hero with a Thousand Faces by Joseph Campbell

Scenes and Sequels: How to Write Page-Turning Fiction. By M. Klassen, 2016.

Creating Character Arcs. K.M. Weiland, 2016.

My Character Page
and all these links are in the Writer's Resources Vault
https://www.subscribepage.com/resource-vault

Chapter 3

Writing Groups

Some people hear "writing group" and immediately cringe or even run like they are being chased by a tiger on fire. This is usually because they have tried a writing group and had a bad experience or they've heard about the bad experiences. I've heard my share of horror stories.

A large critique group in my area is notorious for taking pride in ripping apart the writing merely for the sake of ripping it apart. The feedback is not constructive in the slightest. Consensus is, in that group, that if your writing doesn't have cursing and steamy scenes in it, then you are a prude. You aren't a "real writer" and therefore, not worth their time.

However, I currently participate in two writing groups and love them.

It is hard to spend days, months, or years writing something. You take a piece of your soul and put it into your writing, kind of like a Horcrux. Then people say that you should share it with other people who are going to tell you what is wrong with it!? That is just crazy talk!

Well, here is the deal. People are going to judge the writing and your writing ability when you publish it. Now, if you are just writing for yourself, or for posterity, with no intent to publish, you could skip the writing group. If you have any plans to publish your writing, I highly recommend you find a writing group of some kind. Better to hear of flaws in your writing from people who become friends, than to hear (or not hear) it from readers. A friend will pick your work up again even if the first piece had flaws. A casual reader is less likely to pick up another book if they didn't like the first.

You may say, "I tried a group. It was the most horrible thing I've ever experienced." It likely wasn't the right fit for you. There are many kinds of writing groups. Each individual group has their own personality. It takes time to find one that is right for you.

Critique Group

This is what people usually think of when you say writing group. This type of group is typically 4-6 people. More than that becomes too time-consuming. If the group becomes bigger than that and the meeting space is large enough, the group can be subdivided into 2 or more smaller groups.

Typically, each person gets a copy of the text being read, and one person will read out-loud a certain number of pages or for a certain length of time. Listeners will scribble notes on the page for you to review later. Then they go around a circle verbally highlighting their thoughts on what was read. In my group (since 2 of us are teachers–we like structure and positivity) we require that you say it sandwich style:

- Start with something you like/love about the writing
- Add an area in which the writer can grow (improve)
- End with something positive.

The hardest part of the whole process is that when you are listening to the comments, you are not allowed to speak. You cannot answer if they ask any questions. You can't explain your thinking. You must listen, nod, and take notes. This prevents you from getting defensive. You have to develop a mindset that they are only comments. You will, with time, learn which comments to ignore and which you need to take to heart.

I highly recommend that you try going more than once. The first few times I went to mine I experienced a myriad of emotions: nervousness, excitement, embarrassment, soul-crushing hurt, and elation. I started to learn some things. I started to change my mindset. For a time, I thought I was just an awful writer. (I'm really good at dismissing positive comments and focusing on the negative ones.) One month, I brought a different type of writing. The group loved it! They insisted that I write several short stories with this character. The difference? I believe it was the genre: epic fantasy vs. urban fantasy. This group is not as fond of epic fantasy as they are of urban. Finding the right critique group for what you are writing is critical.

Do not put up with people who are abusive. There is a way to point out areas for you to improve without being insulting or down right rude.

On the other hand, it may *feel* like they are being abusive when you first start out hearing the feedback. So listen to how the critique is phrased to determine if they are being abusive or not. Here is an example:

"This Jenni character is stupid. Why did she run into the woods at night when she knows a serial killer is loose? Really, don't you think that's a little cliché?"

Look at the words this person used: stupid, cliché. And the tone is sarcastic. Now look at this:

"In the first few chapters, Jenni makes some really intelligent decisions, like when she broke up with her cheating boyfriend and when she chose to study for her exam instead of going to a party. Her decision in chapter 9 to go into the woods at night when she knew there was a serial killer on the loose seems incongruous with that character."

Do you see the difference in language and tone? One is helpful and backed up with supporting evidence and one is insulting.

Pay attention to this as you give feedback to others as well. The writer has put their heart and soul into this work, so phrase things gently while remaining honest.

Social Writing Group

This is my favorite kind. I go to my social writing group every week. It is an extremely laid-back group. Usually, anywhere between 8- 18 of us meet at 5pm-ish at a coffee shop. Some show up earlier and some show up later. We go until 9pm-ish. Originally we kept to a schedule. On the first Thursday of the month, we would sit and write. Second Thursday was for brainstorming plot problems. The third Thursday was for critique. The fourth Thursday was a night off. Several of us just came anyway though. Over the last three years of meeting, we've changed it so that we do all those things every week as needed.

The way we handle critiques is much different from what people traditionally do. We print a few copies of a chapter. Then we put them in the middle of the table for someone to pick up, read, and write comments on it. Sometimes after they write comments on the pages, they meet with the person to explain what they meant by their comments, offer suggestions, and brainstorm fixes.

Many nights we write a little and talk a lot. Some might think it is a waste, but I find it energizing. Often, I go home afterward and write. The words flow much easier.

Sit-in Writing Group

I have participated in these during NaNoWriMo. These remind me of the lock-ins that I used to go to as a teenager. Sometimes they go on all night long. I went to one at an IHOP. It started at 9 pm. I tapped out at around 3 am. Others went on until 6 am!

These are simple. Set a time and place. Bring your laptop, tablet, notebook, or whatever you write on. Introduce yourself. Order food, coffee, tea. Write for hours and hours on end. Pause periodically to strike up a conversation if you wish to defog your brain.

This group had word sprints too. This was a kind of gamification of it. The leader of this group would announce a 15 min, 30 min, or 1 hour word sprint. We'd write as much as we could in the given time. At the end she'd call time and we would announce our word count. She had small prizes for the winners. It made it fun and since this was for a rough draft, it was good for getting words on the page.

When the sun came up, we finished our liquid caffeine and went home.

Of course, you could modify this rather extreme form to a shorter, more reasonable form to fit your particular needs. Some groups meet for shorter periods of time. For example, a group in Frisco, TX, meets at a restaurant every Sunday afternoon from 3-6 pm. This is a sit-in where they just write for 3 hours.

Writing Buddy

I would guess that this is the least threatening. This is you and a friend getting together at your homes, a coffee shop, a restaurant, or anywhere to write, brainstorm, problem-solve, or just talk in general about writing.

Online Writing Groups

NaNoWriMo is a great place to meet a myriad of writers online. Particularly during the April and the July NaNos. For those, you get set up in a digital cabin (like a private chatroom) and you get to know one another. You can form your own cabin or ask to be assigned to a cabin with like-minded people. It is great fun! Some people form lasting friendships through these.

There are a bazillion...well okay, hundreds of online places to meet other writers. I've met some really lovely people through Facebook pages like *I am a Writer with Sarah Werner*. There is also Scribophile and Inked Voices. Some of these have monthly fees. There are many more excellent websites.

Twitter and Instagram are good sources of potential critique partners. Twitter has a particularly huge writing community. #amwriting and #writingcommunity will help you find people on both platforms.

How to Find a Writing Group

I found my social writing group through a

website/app called https://www.meetup.com/. It is great for finding writing groups, book club groups, pretty much any kind of group you want to connect with. I found my critique group through the NextDoor app for my neighborhood. You can also find groups online or in-person through Facebook, Twitter, Instagram, or other social media platforms.

You could always start your own writing groups. Put out a plea for members on your favorite medium, like NextDoor, Facebook, Instagram, Twitter, or Meetup. You could meet with them at someone's home, a library, or even online through a program like Zoom or Skype.

In my Writer's Resources Vault, there is a document that gives step by step instructions to set up a writing critique group.

Chapter 4

Alpha and Beta Readers

What is an Alpha Reader?

An alpha reader is the first person or people to read your manuscript. For me, this is my husband, my sister, and my writing group. For you, this might be your siblings, your parents, and friends. I generally recommend you choose someone who is intimately familiar with the writing process and understands story really well. If your mom, dad, or friend is not normally a reader, then do NOT ask them to be your alpha reader. Try to find a writing group if you can, or start one!

Prior to asking an alpha reader to help you, make sure the manuscript you've written is in as good shape as you can get it. You don't want to give them half-thought-out nonsense. They are there not as a co-writer but as someone to help you grow and improve as a writer, so you do your best. Then they can help you improve from there.

If you want feedback on the premise of your novel, you might try typing up the idea and presenting that summary to your alpha reader(s). For my current manuscript, I thought out the plot and sub plot and typed it up. It was a 3 page synopsis. I chose one person from my writing group to read it. She gave me feedback on it and suggestions to strengthen certain plot points. I didn't share it with the whole group of about 10 people because it would be too overwhelming to get suggestions from so many people and I want to get their initial reactions as I write each chapter. If they knew the whole plot ahead of time, it would ruin that response.

What is the Purpose of an Alpha Reader?

This is the person that will give you your first feedback. You might want this person to encourage you. For example, I could write the worst thing ever written and hand it to my mother. I guarantee you her feedback every time would be, "That is great dear!" That feels good, but it is not very helpful. I don't want to keep writing something flawed, so I need more unbiased feedback.

Your alpha reader should be someone who knows something about the kind of writing you are doing. I generally write fantasy and science fiction. Some members of my writing group do not read fantasy, so when I hand them a fantasy story and ask for their feedback, they will sometimes give me a negative response. This is either because I've done something wrong, or because this person is not used to the unique techniques commonly used in fantasy writing.

Find someone that regularly reads the genre of writing that matches your manuscript.

Some authors will give the alpha reader the whole manuscript at once. Other authors will send it out a chapter or a few chapters at a time. I prefer to give it out a chunk at time so if my novel starts to go in a wrong direction, I can adjust the course of it based on alpha feedback. If I send it to alphas all at once and the alphas say it gets bad in the middle, I might have to scrap half the book and rewrite it.

What Kind of Feedback do you Need at this Point?

You need to know if you are going in the completely wrong direction with your writing.

- Plot holes
- Continuity
- Characterization
- Underdeveloped Characters
- Believability
- Underdeveloped plots or subplots
- Unnecessary subplots
- POV choice
- Pacing

- Story structure

Here is a letter that I give to each new alpha reader I enlist. This gives them a pretty clear guide to my expectations for feedback and their purpose.

Dear Alpha Reader,

Thank you so much for volunteering to be an Alpha Reader for me, helping me to become a better writer!

What is an Alpha Reader?

An Alpha Reader is one of the first people to read a story. So the story is far from what it will be in the end. I may make major changes to the story based on my alpha reader feedback from you and others. That is how important your feedback is to me. So again, thank you!

What kind of feedback am I looking for at this point?

The Alpha Reader is not looking for grammatical errors or punctuation errors, they are looking more broadly, at the structural level. Which means, these are the kinds of things I want to know at this point in the process:

Where do you get confused?

What parts do you find unbelievable?

Where do you get bored?

What parts do you love? (So I don't accidentally "fix" it later)

You don't need to tell me how to fix it. (I actually prefer that you didn't.) Just tell me where it feels broken or what feels broken, and I'll figure out how to fix it.

Tell me anything you like, as long as it is constructive; I will not be offended. I am looking for genuine feedback, not a pat on the head saying, "Good job." I've had lots of practice receiving feedback and maintaining friendships afterward. :-)

Here are some example comments:

- *This character seems flat/ has no personality.*
- *I don't really know this character very well.*
- *I hate this character because he is annoying.*
- *I didn't understand who was saying this (arrow to dialogue)*
- *This part goes on too long.*
- *I got bored here. (draw a line, an arrow, or bracket)*
- *This seems out of character for this character.*
- *This part seems contrived.*
- *I love this line/ paragraph.*
- *This ending did not satisfy me.*
- *The setting here is unclear.*
- *Why did _ (character name) _ choose do this instead of ____.*
- *I really liked...*

Basically write anything you are thinking as you read the story!

Thank you again!
~Kathryn

This document is also in the Writer's Resources Vault as a Google Doc which you can copy and adapt for your own purposes.

What is a Beta Reader?

Alpha Readers tend to be writer-type friends while Beta Readers typically are pure reader—no background in writing. They don't write novels, they just really enjoy a good story.

I will give this draft to them all at once. This way I can get more reliable feedback about the pacing of the overall story.

Though they might not speak in technical terms, they give you invaluable feedback. Better that they tell you the beginning was boring now, rather than have potential readers not buy it once it is released.

Beta readers are important because you and your writing peers are sometimes too close to the story after 3-4 revisions. You can't see the forest for the trees.

Beta readers will usually only read the story once and give you feedback. Hopefully at this point the story is close to ready for publication and may only need a little tightening up and tweaking based on this feedback.

Comments from this type of reader might look like:

- The middle gets a bit slow.
- That book wore me out! I couldn't put it down.
- I love [character name].
- I took a break from the story after chapter 7
- The villain is too relatable; I was actually rooting for him to win!

- The story line with [character name] is not very interesting.
- I saw that twist coming back in chapter 12
- That twist didn't make sense.
- The twist was amazing! I knew something wasn't right, but I didn't see that coming!

Finally, after you make the fixes suggested by your Alpha and Beta Readers, you are ready for line edits and agonizing about a single comma for days on end. No, actually please don't agonize about a comma!

Remember though, different people tend to have different definitions for alpha and beta readers. There is no right and wrong. It makes no difference, just get opinions from several different kinds of readers. That's what counts!

Part 2

Road to Publication

Chapter 5

Do I need an Editor?

Do I need an editor?

The short answer is yes.

What kind though? There are lots of editors out there.

People always think of the acquisitions editor of a publishing house and think that's all you need. Perhaps that used to be true. Today...not so much. They've all gotten much more specialized. Now you can hire editors to do different things.

- Developmental Editing Certification
- Copy Editing Certification
- Proofreading Certification
- Continuity Editor

Publishing House Acquisitions Editors

They are the ones who read your manuscript and say yes or no to publishing it. If they reject it, that's it. Don't argue, beg, or send them a revised version of the story. More on that in chapter 11.

They may like your story, but they have to absolutely LOVE your story to accept it.

Additionally, it has to fit within their target for publishing that year. Your dragon story might be amazing, but they may already have three dragon stories in the works this year. They might be looking for something with unicorns or magical cats or something different.

If they accept it, they will often suggest/require some changes to the book title, storyline, characters names, etc. They work with you, not to rewrite and turn your story into something new, but to make your story the best possible version of your story that it can be.

BEFORE you get to that editor, you have to get your story into really good, lovable shape. I promise you, no publishing house editor is going to love any story that has spelling and grammar errors.

The good news is that you can hire these kinds of editors!

Developmental Editors

They give you feedback on the development of your story. Are your characters flat? Is the middle too slow? Are there inconsistencies throughout the story?

Did you foreshadow the twist enough or too much? Did the reveal of the twist happen too late or too early?

This is the first kind of editing you want to do. This is what I call broad brush editing. This editing looks at the whole story at once, big major parts of the story. They are also looking for mixed metaphors, or detailed inconsistencies like this character has a scar on their elbow on page 12 but the scar is on their shoulder on page 87.

Line Editor and the Copy Editor

These are actually two different things but the difference is subtle and varied depending on who you ask. I lumped them together for our purposes. This type of editor looks at the fine details. They've zoomed in at the sentence level. They are looking at it like your English teacher; checking spelling, punctuation, grammar, syntax, word choice and more.
(Syntax is the way you construct your sentences.)

Both of these editors can help you increase your chances of getting published.

So do you need to hire an editor? Yes.

I'm an English teacher and I hire an editor for my writing.

But I know how to write. Why do I need one?
Objectivity.

I can read over my writing 500 times and my mind fills in the gaps so thoroughly that I don't even see my mistakes.

In fiction, I know what my characters mean when they say something. My readers don't know them yet, so I have to make sure the reader will understand them as well. An editor can let me know when I haven't done that well.

If you are curious about editing rates, have a look at the Editorial Freelancers Association (EFA) here https://www.the-efa.org/rates/

Chapter 6

Summaries, Pitches, and Blurbs

There are several types of summaries you'll need to write for your story. You can write these as you need them or sit down and create them all together to pull when you need them. You can write these summaries at any time, but if you do them before your story is even finished, you will certainly want to go back and verify that they still match your story after it has been written.

I don't know about you, but my stories do tend to go off in a direction of their own sometimes.

Right now, I have a story on hold while I write this book. I didn't want to forget my original idea, so I wrote a 3 page synopsis of the story that I had planned.

You will need several different synopses for your novel that will be used for different purposes. The main difference between the various different summaries is the lengths, the audience, and spoilers or no spoilers.

47

Tagline

The target audience for this is the reader or potential reader. This is a 1 sentence marketing phrase. This is meant to grab the reader's attention. This can be used on all kinds of promotional materials. If you self-publish, you'll need this. If you publish traditionally, it is likely that the marketing people will create this.

Length: 1 short sentence
Audience: Potential Readers
Spoilers: No

Logline

This is a 1 sentence summary of your story. The audience for this sentence is people who will potentially buy your manuscript. This is very similar to an elevator pitch.

Length: 1 Longish Sentence
Audience: Agents and Editors
Spoilers: No

Elevator Pitch

Imagine you find yourself riding in an elevator with the publisher of your dreams. You have only the length of an elevator ride to convince him or her to publish your book. This is a 30 second speech that you will want to carefully craft and memorize. It should be one to three sentences long. Write out a dozen versions of it, then choose the best one.

Length: 1-3 sentences
Audience: Agents and Editors
Spoilers: No

Agent Pitch

This is a three to seven minute carefully thought out and memorized speech. Usually at an agent pitch you'll give the three to seven minute pitch, then the agent will spend the remainder of the 10-15 minutes asking you questions about the story.

Describe the plot without spoilers.

There is an excellent post on this topic from Tomi Adeyemi, author of Children of Blood and Bone. Link is in the further reading section.

Length: 3-7 minutes
Audience: Agents and Editors
Spoilers: No

Query Letter Synopsis

This is just a story hook to entice the agent or editor to read the manuscript. The entire letter will be about 400 words or less and only a paragraph of it is the story hook. This should identify the main characters, the conflict, and what sets this story apart from the million

other stories in your genre. More on this in Chapter 8.
Length: less than 400 words
Audience: Agents and Editors
Spoilers: No

Novel Synopsis

Agents and editors will sometime request a synopsis. It should describe the plot, the character arcs and reveal how the conflict is resolved.
Length: 1-2 pages (some will ask for more)
Audience: Editors and Agents
Spoilers: Yes

Book Blurb

This is the summary you'll need for the back of the book.
Length: Less than 300 words
Audience: Potential Readers
Spoilers: No

Further reading about Synopses

Tagline
https://writershelpingwriters.net/2013/09/how-to-write-a-tagline-for-your-book-and-why-you-need-to/

Query Letter
https://www.janefriedman.com/query-letters/

https://query-letter.com/how-to-write-a-query-letter/query-letter-vs-synopsis/

Pitch
http://www.tomiadeyemi.com/blog/how-to-pitch-a-literary-agent-in-5-easy-steps

Synopsis
https://www.janefriedman.com/how-to-write-a-novel-synopsis/

https://query-letter.com/how-to-write-a-query-letter/query-letter-vs-synopsis/

All these links are in the Writer's Resources Vault
https://www.subscribepage.com/resource-vault

Chapter 7

Do I need an Agent?

If you are publishing traditionally, unless you are a lawyer I recommend getting an agent. An agent is an expert in the field of publishing. They know what the norms are and they know how to negotiate a fair book contract. Some publishers won't even look at an unagented manuscript.

How do I get an agent?

You write a query letter and send it to various agents until you find one that loves your story.

How do I find agents to query?

The most common advice I hear is to read the acknowledgments in your favorite books or books similar to yours. Authors will usually thank agents in the acknowledgments. By doing this, you know you are querying agents who represent books similar to yours.

You can also try websites like PublishersMarketplace.com, AgentQuery.com, and QueryTracker.net. You can also try Writers Market if you prefer a paper resource.

What exactly does an agent do for you?

When they get your query letter, they read it and determine if they are interested in your story. They might ask for the first three chapters of your manuscript if they are interested. If they like those three chapters, they'll ask for the full manuscript. Then they decide if they like the story enough to represent it.

If they decide it is not a good fit for them, they'll send you a nicely worded rejection letter. And that is that. Accept it gracefully. Your pride will be wounded, but it is important to remember: This is not a rejection of you; it is a rejection of this particular piece of writing. Often they will encourage you to keep trying and submit other work to them.

The agents might really like your story, but if they don't love it enough to read and work with you on it for 50 billion rereads of it, then they really shouldn't be your agent. You want someone that is massively in love with your story!

If they accept it, congratulations! You have just achieved more than most! Depending on the personality of the agent, they might suggest some changes. As with editors, they are not going to remold your story into something new and reshape it into an unrecognizable blob. Their goal is to help take the story to the next level and make it the best possible version of the story in your head. Some agents will not suggest any changes. It is important that, before you sign any contracts with the agent, you know what kind of person the agent is and what their vision and style is. Some agents communicate a lot with their authors, some barely talk to them. Some agents prefer to communicate by phone and some prefer to communicate by email or video conference. Some are blunt and straightforward, others are gentler. None is right or wrong, it just depends on if your two personalities mesh well.

Once you sign on with an agent, you make changes they suggest, if they suggest any. Then they start querying publishers on your behalf. They know your story and they know publishers. This can make the process a bit faster than if you sent them out because they know which publishers like your kind of story. However, be prepared for a possible long wait. Don't expect a book deal in a week or even a month. I have friends with agents who have been waiting a year or more.

Publishers have massive TBR piles of manuscripts! Plus they do way more than sit around and read manuscripts all day.

If you get a book offer, then you'll be pleasantly surprised!

While you wait, write another book. A good agent will keep you updated on responses from publishers.

The Offer

Once the agent gets one or more book deal offers, they will read the offers. They understand all the lingo in the contracts. If by some miracle, you get more than one offer, the agent can tell you the advantages and disadvantages of each offer. They might even be able to use it for leverage to create a bidding war. Wouldn't that be fun! This is extraordinarily rare though, so don't expect this to happen.

It used to be that publishers would offer something like a $10,000 advance for a book deal. They would give you $10,000 when you signed the contract. Then once the book hit the market you would not get any more money until that $10,000 earned out. Earning out means that enough books are sold to equal that $10,000 in royalties.

The publishing company would hope that the book would earn out in the first year. Once you had earned out that money, only then would you start getting royalty payments every quarter (every 3 months). However, many authors never earn that much on a book. So, from what I understand, publishing companies are not giving out an advance or they are giving much smaller advances. (More on this later)

This information about the advance and royalty

payments is in the contract. If you have a good agent, they can advise you on whether to accept the contract or not. They can negotiate a better deal. While it would be fun to get a $10,000 advance, it might not be best to negotiate that kind of deal. If your book does not earn out the 10k advance, then that publisher has lost money on it and you are less likely to get another book deal with them.

Authors do not usually write one book and then retire on the proceeds of that one book. They usually rely on royalties from many, many books to support themselves so getting more book deals is a priority.

An example short story contract is in the Writer's Resources Vault.

Chapter 8

Pitching to an Agent

This is very nerve-wracking for many authors. This comes in many different forms. One of the shortest and most commonly heard about is the elevator pitch.

You can look on Twitter for Pitch Wars.

For this, pretend you are in the elevator with your dream agent. You have only the time it takes to travel to the 5th floor to tell them about your story and grab their attention. What do you say?

An elevator pitch needs to be a 1-2 sentence summary of your story that's enticing.

Another pitch you might need to do is one at a conference, a face-to-face meeting with an agent. Usually, these last between 10-15 minutes total—two to three minutes of you pitching and the remaining time the agent can ask you questions.

This kind of pitch needs to contain the basics:

- Title
- Word count
- Genre
- Setting
- Main character
- Conflict
- Stakes

Often when you purchase tickets to a conference, a pitch opportunity with one of the agents will be included. Some say it is good practice to listen to pitches, even if you are not yet ready to pitch your story.

You will be given a 10-15 minute time-slot with an agent for your pitch. Keep your pitch to 2-3 minutes, leaving plenty of time to discuss the story, and let the agent ask questions such as:

- How is your story different from others on the market?
- Are you working on any other projects? Is there a sequel? Can this be a stand alone?
- Who are some of your favorite authors?

If you are lucky, they'll ask

- Can you send me the first 3 chapters?
- Can you send me the full manuscript?

Some Advice

Practice your pitch until you are saying it in your sleep. Don't spend half the time off topic, jump right into the pitch. If the agent doesn't request a partial or full read, be open to feedback. They are experts and you should carefully consider any feedback they can give you about your story. This is a great learning experience even if your manuscript is not accepted.

Does my Manuscript Need to be Complete?

Yes! When you meet with the agent, you should have a finished manuscript that has been edited and is as perfect as you can possibly make it.

As a new author, an agent is not going to ask you to write a manuscript on assignment. That comes much later, after you have a number of books under your belt.

Further Reading about Agents

http://www.tomiadeyemi.com/blog/how-to-pitch-a-literary-agent-in-5-easy-steps

https://www.janefriedman.com/pitch-agents-writers-conference/

Chapter 9

Publishing Options

Traditional Publishing House

What goes on in a publishing house? Let's follow a manuscript through the publishing house and find out.

The first person your story will see is a slush-pile reader.

For short stories in magazines, the slush-pile reader is usually a volunteer. If your story is good enough in their eyes, they'll send it up to the editor.

The first rejection letter I got was from one of my favorite magazines. I was proud to have my first rejection letter. (You must celebrate these things, not let it get you down.) I posted it proudly on Twitter. I didn't even realize that it had made it beyond the slush pile until a kind person pointed out that this was signed with the editor's name and wasn't a form letter. I was over-the-moon excited then!

In this business, if you are getting a personalized

rejection letter, you are really close to getting published.

For a big book publishing house, the slush pile reader could be an intern or a junior level agent. In a small publishing house, this will likely be the acquisitions editor. They'll read the query letter. If that is good, they'll read the first chapter. This is why the query letter and the first chapter are so important. If the story is not what their publishing house is looking for, they'll send you a nice form letter or a personalized one. If it does sound like a story the publishing house is interested in, they will request a full manuscript.

If you are getting requests for full manuscripts, then you are close to getting an offer.

If they read your full manuscript and don't think it is quite right for them, they may offer you a letter with feedback to improve your writing. If they like it, they will take it to their team.

Staffing at various publishing houses vary and smaller houses will have people that wear more than one hat. Generally speaking the team consists of:

- Editorial staff
- Legal staff
- Production staff
- Creative department (cover design)
- Sales department
- Subsidiary rights staff (foreign rights and movie rights)
- Publicity staff

- Accounting
- Technology
- Human resources

The marketing people will read it and decide if the manuscript is marketable. If they have already published 4 novels about mermaids this year, they might not want to publish a 5th one because it might not sell as well after so many have already been published. Each member of the team reads the book and gives their recommendation to sign the author or not.

If the team agrees, they put together an offer for the author. Legal staff will draft the offer.

If you, the author, accept the offer, the editor will likely suggest changes to strengthen the story. The creative team will begin to commission the artwork and design the cover layout. Sales will begin drafting a sales strategy.

Publicity will develop publicity materials. They'll start setting up book signings and conference events. You might get a little or a lot of publicity from the publishing house. Don't expect them to do a lot of publicity for you. These days authors are expected to do a lot of their own marketing.

The subsidiary rights staff will see if they can sell your book to publishers in other countries.

They can also talk to movie producers to get your book made into a movie. You might hear about authors having a book in "options" and it sounds like the book is going to be made into a movie. The reality is that options merely means movie people are thinking about making it into a movie. There are many steps in that process.

Accounting will cut a check for your advance if there was an advance negotiated in your contract. They will also prepare for money from your books to roll in so they can send your 10% cut of the sales (or whatever percent was negotiated in the offer). Ten percent is average for traditional publishing.

As you can see, many people work very hard to get your book into the customer's hands, and they each deserve to be paid a fair wage for their part in it. This doesn't even yet take into account all the sales people and bookstore staff that have to be paid for stocking and selling your book. So you might think that a hardcover book priced at $20 would make some decent money after selling 1,000 books. $20,000 right? Nope! Authors usually get 10% so that is only $2,000. So to become the millionaire you might dream of becoming you'd have to sell half a million copies of the book. Most books are lucky to sell 10,000 copies. However, you can always hope to be the lucky person who has the book that hits the market at just the right time with just the right story and sells millions of copies.

Many "overnight success author stories" you hear about were actually 10 years of blood, sweat, and tears…lots and lots of tears, plus endless nights slaving away alone at a desk. (And late nights with a writing group, brainstorming and creating.)

There are also small presses. These are small versions of traditional publishing houses. I are often very niche specific. So if you are having trouble finding the right publisher with the big companies, it might be because the book is too niche and big companies don't have any hope of selling millions of copies of a book about robot mermaids. But perhaps there is a small press that is looking for just that kind of story because their niche is all about robots of all kinds, including robot mermaids. A small press can sell a few thousand copies and still make money off it because they have less overhead than big presses with multiple teams.

Traditional publishing used to be the only way a person could get published, but this is not the case anymore. There are a few other options for publishing books.

Indie Publishing

Indie is short for Independent and is also called self-publishing. This means you are having the book published independent of any company. It used to be that this method of publishing was scoffed at and these authors were viewed as inferior or just not good enough. This view has changed in the last couple of decades. Today indie publishing has boomed and more professionals are recognizing the talent, skill, and dedication of indie authors. Slowly, methods are being put into place to recognize quality indie author writing.

Is it hard to self-publish? Yes, it is a lot of work, but anything worth doing *is* a lot of work. Is it impossible? No. The nice part about this method is the control you have over every aspect of the book.

The disadvantage is that some indie authors don't invest in good editing, so their book is riddled with mistakes. This casts a shadow over the whole indie market.

What are the steps in self-publishing?

There are many different options for indie publishing. One of the most popular options is KDP, Kindle Direct Publishing.

For KDP, the manuscript needs to be in a Word document format. Next you must create a KDP account. This is a step-by-step process through various forms such as your name, address, bank information (so they can pay you royalties), and tax information (because this is a business and you'll have to report your income). If you are a minor, you'll need your guardian to do this portion.

In the setup process for the book, you'll select the book size you want, the page quality and color, the binding type, and more. Typical paperback book size is often 5.25" x 8".

There are two main paper back sizes trade paperback books and mass market books.

Mass market books are the smallest, usually approximately 4" x 6". The paper quality might be lower than a trade paperback depending on the publisher.

Trade paperback books are smaller than a hardback book but larger than mass market books. They usually average 6" x 9" in size. These books will often have a higher quality, slightly thicker paper.

You can choose white or cream paper. There are options for color or black and white on the interior pages. There are choices for the cover as well. For binding, you can choose various qualities of glue binding, which vary in price accordingly. Once all the choices are made, KDP will give you a template which shows the measurements and requirements for correct formatting for your manuscript and your book cover.

Formatting

You'll need to format your manuscript. If you are using Scrivener software, you'll want to compile it into RTF format and open it in Word. (Scrivener is a software program many authors use to outline and compose their story.)

If your manuscript is already in Word, then you can simply begin configuring it into the necessary format.

Each page will need headers. The left page header normally is the name of the book. The right hand page headers varies. It could be your author name, a chapter title or chapter number. The footer will contain the page number starting with chapter 1, not the front matter (title page, etc.).

You'll also need to adjust the margins. The KDP

template will let you know the measurements. One of the measurements is the gutter which is the side of the page that gets glued in the spine, so you'll need a little extra lengths for that side.

Cover Design

KDP gives a template with measurements for each part of the cover: front, spine, and back. If you have a program like Adobe Photoshop, you can use that or there are a few free websites that can be used to create the cover. Any program that allows you to convert the file to .jpg and .png will work.

I highly recommend going to the bookstore or going online and looking at comp books—books that are comparable or similar to yours—so you can study the design of those novels. Look at the comp books that are most successful. Look at the fonts that other authors use. What kinds of images do they use? Are there images or is it just words? Are the images on the cover real photos, paintings, or clip-art?

Use these as inspiration, do not copy anyone's cover too closely. I've seen this with Victoria Aveyard's book, Red Queen. That book was wildly successful, so others looked at her covers that depicted a bloody crown, and copied it to some degree. Suddenly more books hit the market with crowns on them, probably in hopes of tricking people into thinking it was another Victoria Aveyard book. Many people, like me, are turned off by someone who tricks or misleads others in that manner. Part of that was just a marketing trend as with The Cruel

Prince by Holly Black. There is a crown on the cover, but nobody would mistake that for Aveyard's book because there are significant differences in style. Make your design unique, not a copy of others.

Something you must be concerned with is copyrights. You can't just pull a random image off the Internet to use for your book cover. You must make sure the image you decide on is used with permission for profit. You can go to websites such as Pixabay and find images available for free. Check the license though. Some require attribution, some can't be used for profit. Vector Stock is a website that offers images inexpensively.

Many people are willing to work with you, if you only seek permission. A friend of mine found an image she loved and wanted to use on the cover of her book. She tracked down the owner of the image and asked for his permission to use the image. He gladly gave it. I think she sent him a copy of her book in thanks.

I found a drawing of a dragon that I loved on Etsy. I contacted the artist and asked her permission to use it on my blog as the blog header. She gave me permission to use it on the condition I kept her Instagram handle on the image. I happily obliged.

Images or drawings need to be 300 pixels per inch or higher in order to look good when printed out on the book cover. Once you have all the elements laid out, you'll want to merge the layers and convert the finalized book cover design into .png for ebook and .jpeg for paperbacks.

There is also the option to hire a professional to design your book cover. You can find some on Fiverr, Reedsy, or a similar type site. If you only hire a professional for only one thing, hire a cover designer. No one will buy your book if the cover doesn't look enticing. A good designer will charge at *least* $300 and an experienced one will charge much more than that.

ISBN

Each book type will need a separate ISBN number. What that means is that your paperback book will need an ISBN number and large print version (if you make one of those) will need a different ISBN number. When you make significant changes to the book, like a new cover, then you'll need a new ISBN. Ebooks require an ASIN number which you don't have to purchase. This is a number assigned to the book by the selling platform, like Amazon.

Purchase your ISBNs from Bowker Link. (https://www.bowkerlink.com/corrections/common/hom e.asp) This is the only reliable source for them.

Other sites selling them are brokers or scams. They will sometimes sell the same number to multiple people, which gets *really* messy!

From Bowker Link, you can buy 10 numbers for the most cost effective route. You won't need 10 now, but you'll need more later. If you change the book significantly or you write more books, you can use those other numbers later.

KDP does offer ISBNs but then they own the number and they are considered the publisher   The listing will have CreateSpace Independent Publishing as the publisher. Also book sales are tracked by the ISBN number. If you decide later that you want to publish on another platform, you will need to buy an ISBN and your sales will start at zero again, as if it were a brand new book. If you use the KDP ISBN number, you cannot get a Library of Congress Number, which you'll need if you want your books on the shelves of a library.

If you like control, you want to buy it yourself. If you decide to "go wide" and offer the book on other platforms, you'll want to own that ISBN. Once you have the number for your book there are sites that will create a barcode for you. It will be in an .eps format which can be added as a picture to your book cover.

Blurb

The blurb is the summary on the back of the book. You will need to write several different summaries for various different purposes. The one on the back of the book should introduce the genre, setting, conflict, and the main characters. It should not talk about anything that happens after the midpoint of the story, nor should it contain any spoilers. Do not include the death of any characters unless it happens in the first chapter or prior to the start of the story.

You might also have quotes from beta readers

that are raving about your story.

Author Bio

You will need to write one or more author bios for the back of the book or the book flap and for various social media platforms. Usually there is a word limit or a character limit. Quite often the limit is 150 characters. They are traditionally written in 3rd person, not first person. Here is the bio I wrote for my first short story publication. I had a 50 word limit to work within.

Kathryn Fletcher is an English teacher who lives in Dallas, Texas. She will soon graduate with her Masters of Library Sciences. She lives with her husband, son, and a menagerie of animals including a hedgehog. Kathryn is a quilter, painter, and an all-around nerdy, creative type. QuillAndBooks.com

Social Media Bios

Here is my Instagram bio:

A book nerd, English teacher, and published writer fueled by mocha coffee. I write SFF stories. quillandbooks.com Quillandbooks@gmail.com #amwritingfantasy #infp

Twitter bio:

A fantasy writer, blogger, mom, wife, reader, lover of words, teacher & #mls student

Facebook bio:
*I am a fantasy writer fueled by mocha coffee, tea,
and dark chocolate. I blog at QuillandBooks.com*

Each one is different, but one thing the social
media bios all have in common is that I always include
my blog. This is the heart and soul of my platform. I'll
talk more about that in the Social Media chapter.

Hybrid Publishing

If this were a simple world, those would be your
two choices, but thankfully we don't live in a simple
world. There is also Hybrid Publishing. This actually has
many different names like "assisted publishing" and a
myriad of variations on that. There are a multitude of
definitions and a multitude of models for hybrid
publishing.

Some hybrid publishing houses will offer various
services like a menu. They are essentially a services
broker. If you need an editor, the hybrid publishing
house has one or more on staff or freelancers they use
and trust. If you need a cover, they have designers for
you with experience creating book covers. If you need
your book formatted for paperback or ebook, they have
people in house that do that. You pick and choose which
services you want to use from them. This gives you total
control, but a lot of upfront cost for you.

Some hybrid publishers do require you to send in a query letter for them to accept or not. Their name will be on the book too, so it makes sense that they want to have quality control. They do take a financial risk on your book by paying for the services your book needs or a portion of the services. Next they publish the book and pay you royalties, usually a larger royalty than a traditional publisher but less than if you had self-published. It is less hassle for you, more choice, and possibly less profit.

Some hybrid publishers are starting to shoulder more of the upfront cost and taking more of the royalties, like the traditional publishers, but not as big of a percentage.

Do your research. Be absolutely clear about the expectations on both sides. Check their reputation. I've known many people that got scammed by a hybrid press.

Bottom line: Research anyone you plan to pay.

Vanity Press

Vanity Press publishing is often frowned upon strongly. Long ago, before self-publishing was a common practice, the only options were to publish traditionally or publish through a vanity press. The companies took no financial risk on the author. The author paid for everything. This was before print on demand. Books were run on the printing press in batches of hundreds or thousands. So the author had to purchase something like 2000 books and then had to sell them to make their money back. There are some people out there that think self-publishing is nothing more than vanity press with a new name. It is not at all true, but you may run into this opinion.

Summary of Publishing Options:

Traditional

- Hard to get your manuscript accepted
- No upfront cost
- Less hassle after you close a deal
- Less control throughout the process
- Decisions are in the hands of industry experts
- Higher exposure because they can be carried in all bookstores
- Some marketing is done for you, but you are still responsible for some
- Typically 7-10% Royalties
- Your book is eligible for all kinds of awards (which equals exposure and sales)

Self-Publishing

- You have total control throughout the process
- A lot of upfront cost for you
- Many decisions to make
- You take all the risks

- You do all the marketing or hire it out
- Typically 35-70% royalties
- Your book is eligible for some awards

Hybrid Publishing

- May or may not need to query
- You have some control
- Shared upfront costs
- Shared risks
- You are doing all the marketing or hiring it out.
- Typically ...there is no typical here! Sometimes the royalties are similar to self-published other times it is 50%. Usually higher than traditional publishing.
- Your book is eligible for some awards

Further Reading on Publishing

ISBNs
https://selfpublishingadvice.org/isbns-for-self-published-books/

Hybrid Publishing
https://blog.reedsy.com/hybrid-publishers/

Pros and Cons to Different Publishing Options
https://www.thecreativepenn.com/self-publishing-vs-traditional/

Self-Publishing Checklist
and all these links are in the Writer's Resources Vault
https://www.subscribepage.com/resource-vault

Chapter 10

How do I Write a Query Letter?

First, when should you start querying? When you have finished the book.

I've talked to a lot of new writers who say, "I'm about halfway done with my manuscript, so I've started to send out query letters." My eyes nearly pop out of my head when I hear that. It's great to think ahead but that is putting the horse before the cart for several reasons. One, what if you get 90% in and you realize that something doesn't work and you get stuck or have to go back and do a complete rewrite? Maybe you have to add or remove a whole plot line or character. Now you are querying something that may or may not drastically change.

Two, let's say you send the query letter with the first 3 chapters. The publisher or agent likes it. They ask for a "Full," which means a full manuscript. Then what? Tell them they have to wait a couple months until you can complete it? While they are waiting for you to finish, they might find a story they like better AND is already complete. That is very likely to cause you to miss out. Finish the manuscript, revise, give it to alpha readers, revise, and give it to beta readers, edit, and then query.

While you wait for responses from agents or publishers, start on your next project.

So How do I Write a Query?

For a short story, the idea is to keep it brief. Introduce yourself and let the story speak for itself. It is a very good idea to do a little research and find out the name of the acquisitions editor. Many websites will put it right on the page with all the query information. Some don't make it quite as easy. A Google search for the information is not too hard, though.

Always follow the format on the query page. Some places do blind submissions and require that no identifying information be on the manuscript. Other places require standard format. (See Further Reading on Query Letters at end of this chapter)

Here is an example of one I sent out:

Dear [Editors],

Attached is my short story, "Desperate Trolls Call for Desperate Measures" (3700 words). This story is about a boy with Autism trying to save his neighborhood from a troll. It earned Honorable Mention in the L. Ron Hubbard Writers of the Future Contest.

I am a 6th grade English teacher and a Master of Library

and Information Science student at the University of North Texas. I
have not yet published any stories.

> *Thank you for taking the time to read my submission.*
> *Respectfully,*
> *[Your actual name, not a pen name]*

To be honest, I played with sending it out with a longer summary initially. Then I learned it is better to let the story speak for itself. I only put a one sentence summary in after that. Some people say that you don't need to say anything in the way of a summary. I wanted to with this story because it is about a boy with Autism, which is highly sought after now in this market. (Stories with underrepresented populations, such as minorities and people differently-abled)

Before you start to write a bunch for stories trying to capture a specific market, please take the advice of "write what you know." I have worked with dozens of students over the years who have Autism and I'm trained in special education, so I know about Autism and how it exhibits in many students. I also had several sensitivity readers check it for anything offensive or wrong.

Here is another example:

Dear [editor's name],

> *Attached is my short story, "Locks of Grief" (2507 words).*
> *One of my short stories earned Honorable Mention [writing contest] and was published in [magazine name]. I am an active member of a writing group and a critique group. I am a 6th grade English teacher.*

Thank you for taking the time to read my submission. I hope you enjoy it.

> *Respectfully,*
> *[Real name]*
> *Byline: Kathryn Fletcher*
> *https://quillandbooks.com/about-me/*

This query has no underrepresented populations, so I didn't feel the need to include anything about the story. Be sure to include, as I did in the second paragraph, any honors or publications to your name. You also want to include a tiny bit about yourself especially if it is relevant to your story or writing ability. If your job doesn't relate to writing, don't list it. Don't worry, it's okay. If you don't yet have any honors or publications yet, that is okay too. Editors like to discover new authors. All they really care about is a good story. Give them that, and someone will give you a chance to shine.

One difference between short story submission and novel manuscript submission is with short stories, you must submit to only one editor at a time. Very few magazines allow simultaneous submissions. I've gotten responses back in as little as a few days. Sometimes it takes 3 weeks for a response.

Contests are different. The Writers of the Future contest allows simultaneous submissions. Look at the contest rules to see if the contest you are entering allows simultaneous submission. Writers of the Future is a quarterly contest. I heard from them around four months after submitting.

Writing a Novel Query Letter

Novel queries are a bit more involved.
Some elements you should include in your letter are:

- The agent or editor's name
- Why you are submitting to them.
    - You enjoy other books they've published
    - They publish books similar to yours
    - Maybe you met the agent at a conference and they asked you to submit to them!
- Genre of your story
- Word count
- Title & subtitle if applicable
- A short synopsis of your book (100-200 words)
- A short bio of yourself and your qualifications to write this story if applicable. (less than 100 words)
- If you have a platform with a significant following, include it. (tens of thousands of followers or more)
- Thank them for their time.

The whole letter should be around a page long, no more than 400 words in all.

With books, you *can* do simultaneous submissions, but do not query 40 agents or editors all at once. It is best to send it to two or three to begin with. If you are lucky, they'll request a "partial" which usually means the first three chapters. They will tell you how much they want.

Then they'll either request a "full" which means a full manuscript, or they'll send a rejection letter. They might give you feedback on it. Then you can consider making suggested changes to the manuscript based on that feedback.

A friend of mine has an agent and is currently doing a rewrite of the beginning of the story based on feedback that the agent has been getting from editors. If she had sent the manuscript out to 40 editors at once, then she'd have a great deal fewer editors that she could send her manuscript to after the changes.

Send your query letters out in small batches.

Also, keep track of your queries. I use a spreadsheet. There are some websites and apps that you can use to keep track of them as well. I keep track of:

- Date sent
- Story Name
- Publication
- Editor's name
- Date of Response
- Accepted/Rejected
- Notes

Another tab on my submission tracker sheet is my list of places to submit. On this sheet I keep track of:

- Publishing company
- Link to website
- Submission guidelines
- Pay rate
- Notes

In the notes section, I write down if I see that they are closed to submission until such-and-such date or "as of Jan 3, 2020 closed to submission" and highlight it. This way I can pay close attention and come back to them when the window opens again.

Some months are really good times to submit and some months are slower. When editors and agents go through a busy season because of big projects they are working on, they'll close submissions for a time.

Remember, editors and agents don't just sit around all day reading manuscripts. The majority of their job is working with authors they've already signed. So it might take a long time for them to respond to your query. Try to be patient. And above all, if you get a rejection letter, be graceful. Do not send them a scathing email telling them what a fool they are to not publish your book. Publishing is a relatively small industry and editors talk.

Further Reading on Querying

Manuscript Formatting
https://www.sfwa.org/2005/01/manuscript-format/

Query Letters
https://www.janefriedman.com/query-letters/

https://www.writersdigest.com/online-editor/the-10-dos-and-donts-of-writing-a-query-letter

My Submission Tracker Form
and all these links are in the Writer's Resources Vault
https://www.subscribepage.com/resource-vault

Chapter 11

Letters

Acceptance Letter

If you get an acceptance letter or an offer, Congratulations! Read it carefully. You might get an offer that isn't fair. I've heard of some publishers that try to take away all your story rights indefinitely. This is when it helps to have an agent that can read and understand the offer, and if necessary negotiate a better contract for you.

Don't immediately call your day job and give your notice. If you were lucky and offered a nice advance, great! But it has to earn out before you get any more money. That could be a year or more, depending on how well your book sells. Many books never earn out the advance. If it doesn't earn out, your chances of getting another book deal is diminished. So hang onto that day job for a little while. How long? Get two or three books under your belt to live off the royalties.

Rejection Letter

If you have thin skin, or you're emotionally devastated by rejection, then this might not be a very easy path for you. (Honestly though, it is not an easy path for anyone.) But you can learn to receive rejection and criticism with grace. The writing community online is an amazing support group!

If you have written a story and sent it off, then congratulations! You are a brave person and regardless of the outcome, you should be proud of yourself. I wrote a whole novel manuscript and several short stories before I felt I had something worth trying to publish.

I heard a story from Mary Robinette Kowal on Writing Excuses.

She had a story she didn't think was good enough for her dream magazine X, so she sent it off to magazine Y instead. It was accepted and published. Later the publishing editor of magazine X saw it and told her, "I wish you had sent this to me, I would have published it."

Can you imagine? Your dream publisher...missed because you lacked faith. So, the moral of this story is send your work to your dream publisher first!

That is what I did. I sent my best short story to my dream magazine, fully expecting a rejection because really who gets an acceptance letter on the first go? As expected, a week or so later, I got the rejection letter. I was not at all sad. I was actually excited to have my first rejection letter. It was a rite of passage. You are now part of a club...sort of. Be proud! I was. It was nicely phrased even. So I posted a snapshot of my rejection email on Twitter.

Then someone told me that this was not just any rejection; it was a rejection letter from the chief editor. I had made it through the slush pile and gotten a personalized rejection, not the form letter rejection! To get a personalized rejection is HUGE in this industry! It means that your writing is almost to the level it needs to be to get published.

I sent out the story to more magazines on my wish list. After about a half dozen or so rejections, I finally got a yes!

Most publishers are completely digital now. Many Magazines use a nice program called Moksha. This is an online queue for the stories. Once you've submitted a story through this program it will tell you what your place in line is and an estimated time of feedback.

Why might a story get rejected?

If a story is not formatted correctly, it will automatically get rejected without being read by anyone. For example, they may ask you to submit a blind manuscript, so they are not biased one way or another by the name on the manuscript. Others want your name on each page. So be meticulous about reading the submission guidelines for each submission you make. Many publishers will ask that you submit with the generally accepted standard format. (Link to this format in the Vault)

Some publishers will ask for slight changes though, so read all their requirements.

Other reasons for rejection may include story strength. Be prepared to hear something along the lines of "I really liked your story called ____ but it just didn't grab me." That is the form letter format for short stories. Not very helpful is it? When I see that I think, maybe this just wasn't their type of story or maybe I don't have quite enough polish on the story. Between each submission I usually give my short story another read-through. I'll find one or two things to tweak. I decide that this sentence or that paragraph really can be cut. My final story may look a lot different from my rough draft and even significantly different from the draft I sent out. I even sent it to a New York Editor that C.C. Finley recommended on Twitter. I paid her a lot more to edit the story than I ever could have gotten paid for selling the story. The way I saw it, it was a learning experience. She gave me some really strong (but nice) feedback. Worth every penny if you ask me!

How do you get through the pain of rejection?

Know that everyone gets rejected at some point in their life. Authors deal with rejection a lot.

So how do you go about processing this rejection? It helps to remember that you are certainly not alone. Periodically, you can surf the internet in search of author heroes who were also rejected back in the day. Here are a few examples:

J.K. Rowling's book Harry Potter was rejected 12 times before Bloomsbury picked it up. I read about Rowling in my Library Science textbooks (Literature for Youth). Her books convinced the publishing industry that a children's book can be that much of a money maker. Since then children's books and YA books have had much greater investments.

Stephen King's Novel Carrie was rejected 30 times before being published by Doubleday.

In his book called On Writing, King said that he used to keep his rejections pinned to the wall until he gained too many, so he used a nail to pin them on. I've started my own collection of rejection letters. So far a thumb tack is sufficient to hold my rejection letters. I look forward to switching to a nail one day. It may seem weird, but for me it is a matter of pride in the fact that I'm doing something. That takes guts and I hope that one day it will pay off.

Brandon Sanderson had a long, difficult journey to publication. You can read all the details on his website if you wish. (link in Further Reading)

He wrote 5 books just for practice. Then he wrote *Elantris*, but it didn't get published for a long time after writing it. He collected rejection after rejection, the feedback saying it was too long. He wrote several manuscripts that were aimed at the current market (aka shorter) and hated them. After many years of trial and error and rejection, Sanderson finally got a book deal for Elantris.

James Patterson, author of *The Thomas Berryman Number*, got 31 rejections from publishers before he sold his first manuscript. Then he got an award for best debut novel.

The author of *A Wrinkle in Time*, Madeleine L'Engle got 26 rejections from publishers before her first book deal.

Lemony Snicket's first book was rejected 37 times.

Meg Cabot kept rejection letters in a bag under her bed. Eventually the bag got so heavy she couldn't lift it anymore.

The thing these authors all have in common is that they never gave up. "A professional writer is an amateur who didn't quit." — Richard Bach

Keep writing! Don't stop and sit around waiting for the rejection letters to roll in. Write your next story. So when a rejection letter comes in, you can tell yourself, "Well, there is always this story. Maybe this one will work.

According to an article by Amy Morin (author of "13 Things Mentally Strong People Don't Do") says that strong people handle rejection by:

1. Acknowledge your emotions. Rejection hurts, no matter who you are or what you have done or how wonderful your book is. Remember that the rejection is a rejection of the story, not a rejection of *you*.

2. View rejection as evidence that you are putting yourself out there and pushing yourself. Success does not normally fall into one's lap.

3. Treat yourself with compassion. *Forbid negative self-talk.* When you repeat something over and over, you start to believe it. I suggest you find a phrase that is encouraging and not bitter, no matter how tempting it is to become negative. Try something like:

> "Next time"
> "This wasn't a good fit"
> "The right agent or publisher is out there"

My husband always reminds me of this SNL skit when I have to do something brave: "I'm good enough, I'm smart enough, and doggone it, people like me!" You could change it to "My writing is improving every day. I will keep working towards my goal, and doggone it, my writing will be recognized one day!!"

4. Refuse to let rejection define you. It is very important to keep reminding yourself that the rejection is not of you as an author. It is a rejection of this one piece of writing, from that particular magazine or publishing company.

The rejection letters are normally worded politely. They'll say something like "Thank you for letting me read your story but it didn't quite grab me." This is NOT secret code for, "Your writing is garbage.

You will never be a published author, so give up now." It could be a perfectly good piece of writing, but it might not be a good fit for their niche.

5. Learn from rejection. I shopped around one of my stories quite a bit in adult markets before I finally decided to give the youth market a try. The first youth magazine I submitted to snatched it up. I learned from this experience how important querying the right market really is.

Further Reading About Rejections

5 Ways Mentally Strong People Deal with Rejection
https://www.inc.com/amy-morin/5-ways-mentally-strong-people-deal-with-rejection.html

Best Seller Rejection Stories
http://www.litrejections.com/best-sellers-initially-rejected/

https://snicket.fandom.com/wiki/Daniel_Handler

https://lithub.com/the-most-rejected-books-of-all-time/

https://brandonsanderson.com/euology-my-history-as-a-writer/

http://mentalfloss.com/article/53235/how-stephen-kings-wife-saved-carrie-and-launched-his-career

All these links are in the Writer's Resources Vault
https://www.subscribepage.com/resource-vault

Part 3

Author Life

Chapter 12

Authorpreneur

What are Royalties?

Royalties are your share of the income from sales of your book.

With traditional publishing you can expect to receive between 7% and 25% of the cover price for your book. With self-publishing you can get up to 70% of the cover price. Here is Amazon's formula: (Royalty rate x list price) – printing costs = royalty

There are a ton of variables though. With a traditional publishing deal, you might move more units because of bookstore shelf space in major book retailers.

One secret to making enough money to make writing books a full time job that will support you and your family is to be prolific. Some people take this to the extreme and produce 2-4 books per year. I don't know about you but this is not something I could do. Here is the math behind that idea.

Let's say you publish a book and sell enough to make $100 per month. (Many places pay out every quarter. Some pay twice a year. It varies.) We are also going to pretend that sales are consistent, which they rarely are in real life. So one book, $100 per month. When you have 2 books out, you might pull in another hundred a month. So now you have $200 per month income. Even traditionally published authors can rarely live off of one book's royalties. The average author makes around $20,000 per year. The exception is JK Rowling and Brandon Sanderson. Even they haven't stopped writing and creating. Sanderson still teaches at a university in Utah in addition to publishing new books each year.

Taxes

Once you have a book published, you are now self-employed. So, don't forget to pay income tax quarterly or set aside a percentage of your royalties to pay taxes annually.

Hobby or Authorpreneur

Decide your "why" for publishing. Was it your dream to become published? Now you are published and you are happy. Are you writing to share your stories and making money is a bonus?

Or are you planning to make this a business? If you plan to make a living off your writing, you have to have a business mindset at least part of the time, especially if you are self-publishing. I'm not saying you have to write to the market and sell your soul for the almighty dollar. I'm saying you need to approach decisions with your authorpreneur business in mind. You need a plan. There are several very good books in the further reading section that can help you develop this business plan.

Further Reading about Authorpreneurship

You are a Writer by Jeff Goins

Successful Self-Publishing by Joanna Penn

How to Make a Living with your Writing by Joanna Penn

Business for Authors by Joanna Penn

KDP Paperback Royalties
https://kdp.amazon.com/en_US/help/topic/G201834330

Turbo Tax article on Paying Taxes
https://turbotax.intuit.com/tax-tips/self-employment-taxes/a-tax-cheat-sheet-for-kindle-ebook-self-publishing/L4chgec1V

All these links are in the Writer's Resources Vault
https://www.subscribepage.com/resource-vault

Chapter 13

Social Media

Do I Need an Author Website?

I have heard several podcast episodes and listened to live interviews of editors on this question. The answer each time has been pretty much the same: No it is not a prerequisite for getting a book deal. However, it can help.

Eventually, you *are* going to want to have a website. If you get a book deal with a publisher, they will likely ask you to create one. I can't say I have ever seen a currently living author that doesn't have a website. Some authors have a simple landing page that gives a blurb about the author, a list of books published, and links to social media.

Other authors like myself have a more extensive website that include a blog. With a blog, an author can create a following that will turn into sales when your book is published. So if you have a blog with a following, it can certainly help you. If your following is large enough *and* you have a great story, it can help you get your book published. But if you don't like to blog, don't waste your time doing something you don't enjoy doing. I love to blog as a resource that can help other people find good books to read and learn the writing craft. This does cut into my time to write other things, like this book.

Facebook, Twitter, Instagram, Snapchat, oh MY!

How about all the other social media, do you need that? Like the website issue, you probably should get on one or more, but it is not absolutely required. Building a following can help you. Media like Facebook, Twitter, Instagram, and Snapchat can certainly help your book gain exposure and it allows readers to connect with you. Do you need all of those? No. If you don't have any social media accounts, I would choose one and learn that one. Once you learn that platform, add another until you reach an amount or limit that you think you can handle.

Personally, I use Facebook and Instagram frequently. I peruse Twitter on occasion, but I've never really connected with it because of how the navigation is and it used to have a really limited word count. I still have the account and over a thousand followers on it. I tried Snapchat briefly, but I think I'm too old to connect with it. To each their own! Facebook and Instagram are my two main platforms in addition to my blog.

Guidelines for Online [Promotion]

1. Read and respect the rules set by the groups. If it says no self-promoting...Then don't promote there. Be in the group and make friends. Then later you can more organically let people know that you have a book for sale

2. Follow the 80/20 rule. Research shows it is most effective to create 80% of posts to inform, entertain, or otherwise unrelated to promotion of your book. 20% of the time you can post some kind of promotional material on your feed.

3. The main idea of social media is to connect with other people. Always be polite! If you are being antagonized, don't engage. Do comment on people's posts. Quite often I will comment and then they follow my account. I have made many online friends in this manner.

Email List

You want to start building an email list so that when you release another book, you can tell the people who already know and trust you. People that like your writing on social media and sign up for your email list are more likely to buy your book when it comes out. You might say that it could just be an announcement on Facebook or Instagram. Problem is that you don't control those. Not all of my Facebook friends can see my posts.

Algorithms change and we can't do anything about that. But if I have their email address, I can guarantee that all of them will see it.

This email list can be built by having a sign up form on your webpage. So all the work you put in selling your first book can be used to build momentum for each of your following books.

Chapter 14

Now What?

Other resources

Let me point you to my blog. QuillAndBooks.com As I learn more about this business, I'll share what I learn there. Earlier this year, I delved into writing description. Later this year, I plan to take a look at outlining a novel. From there I will take you on a journey as I write my novel which is based on my short story published here: http://youthimagination.org/

I follow other writers as well. Some of these are:

- KM Weiland has a blog that is a great resource. (Link in Vault)
- Joanna Penn is another source of information I find useful. (Link in Vault)

- *I am a Writer with Sarah Werner* is a lovely facebook group in which I've found many friends.

What else can I do to learn more about this business of writing?

First, read as much as you can. You need to read like a writer though. You might even read a book like a reader, then go back and reread the book with a writer's eye. Examine why you liked or disliked the book. How did the author accomplish this? Right now, I'm 80% into a book I'm not liking. I took a step back and examined why it was that I felt bored and didn't really care about the characters. I've stayed with the book because the author has a fascinating magic system. When I looked back at the story to examine why I was a bored reader, I realized the main character was merely reacting to everything. At 80% into the book, she had no goal other than to learn how to use magic. Her future self is telling the story to a story collector. The exiled character is preparing to do something interesting, but I've realized that it is going to take the author one or two more books to get to that point. So Nope! Sorry. I've learned from this book to give the character a strong purpose or goal to keep readers engaged.

Go to conferences. I learned a ton from attending conferences. Four years ago I couldn't afford to attend the big DFW Writing Conference. So instead I went to a smaller one that was a few hours from my home. My friend Randi and I hopped into the car, drove, and had a blast. It was held in 3 conference rooms. They had editors, publishers, and authors there to talk to us about the business of being an author.

One of my favorite conferences was Lone Star Ink in Dallas, Texas. David Farland came. I actually got to meet David Farland! I devoured all the words he had to say about what he's learned over his long career. One of the most fascinating thing he talked about was getting into an alpha wave state while writing creatively. Farland also taught us about his methods of world building. It was an exhilarating two days.

We also got to hear a New York Agent give all kinds of advice, which I've shared with you in this book.

Books

You shouldn't try to improve all your skills all at once. That is what caused me to stop writing for about 10 years.

Pick an area you want to focus on for a few months or a year and work to improve it. Start by reading a book on the area you choose.

Talk to Authors

Connect with other writers on social media. Twitter has a massive group of writers that use the #writing community. There are a lot of people who do "follow for follow" meaning if you follow them, they will follow you. These are simply vanity numbers. Your follower count will go up but most of those people won't interact with you. Don't worry too much about followers, just get on there and be friendly. Follow only people who post things you find interesting. If they find your comments and posts interesting, they'll follow you back organically.

Podcasts

Outside of reading books, I think this has been the most informative learning outlet. Some podcasts speak directly about writing. One of my favorites is Sarah Rhea Werner's Write Now Podcast. She, in recent years, transitioned from writing as a side hustle to her main hustle.

Another favorite of mine is Writing Excuses. I've been listening to this one for perhaps ten years. This was the first podcast I listened to ever. This podcast is hosted by Brandon Sanderson, Mary Robinette Kowal, Dan Wells, and Howard Taylor. All four are published authors. Mary Robinette Kowal won a Hugo award and Nebula award this year for her novel The Calculating Stars.

Sarah Rhea Werner also produces an audio-drama called Girl in Space which has been wildly popular. Audio-dramas have become popular in recent years. There are dozens of excellent dramas to choose from for inspiration and to study for their craftsmanship. I love Girl in Space because I find the main character so relatable as an introvert. Werner blends action with moments of introspection on life and the human condition. I've learned a lot from listening to this series 3-4 times and examining what she did right with this story.

Podcastle is a publication that produces audio versions of short stories. They love stories centered on different cultures but with a fantasy or fairytale twist.

From Side Hustle to Going Full Time

Choosing the path of becoming an author is not an easy one. I've known several people that have quit their jobs to become a full time author with no publications to their name. This is not necessarily a wise move. It has been done before, but often this is contingent upon a parent or spouse that can carry all household expenses indefinitely.

It is much more common to work full time to pay the bills and work toward becoming an author as a side hustle. They work on their writing in the wee hours of the morning, burn the midnight oil, work during lunch breaks, or all of those. Many have done this successfully.

My Parting Advice

Writing is not an easy road, but it is one rife with joyous moments. You hold in your hands and your brain the ability to create, to transmit your ideas into the brains of others. (Okay, I sound like a mad scientist now!) How cool is that though?!

You will face a great deal of rejection but the best advice I've heard bears repeating: "Professional authors are simply aspiring authors who did not give up."

Ignore the trolls and find a group of people who will support you and help you grow. Groups tend to grow together and publish together. If you don't find an existing group you mesh well with, form your own. Over time, you and your group will learn and one by one you'll get published. I've seen this happening in my groups and I've heard the same about other groups.

You've read this book, so I know you have the mindset of a learner! You will do well with this mindset. I wish you the best of luck on your journey. Stay in touch!

If you found this book useful and informative, please leave a 5 star review on Amazon and tell your friends about this book.
Thank you so much!

Sign up for "Letters from Kathryn" so are the first to get updates on new books, blog posts, and other opportunities. To subscribe to my Letters from Kathryn emails use this QR code or link

https://www.subscribepage.com/lettersfromkathryn

Here is the Writer's Resources Vault QR Code
https://www.subscribepage.com/resource-vault

It is important to me that this book is practically perfect in every way. No matter how many people check over books, mistakes can still happen, so please let me know if you find anything that needs to be fixed. kathryn@quillandbooks.com

Acknowledgments

Thank you to the students who inspired me to write this book!

Thank you to my husband, Jesse, for the sacrifices you've made to help me get this book done. I couldn't have done this without your support and more importantly, your belief in my ability. I love you! And thank you for formatting this book!

Thank you, Levi, for letting Mom work on the computer with only a *few* interruptions.

Extra special thanks to my editor, Beverly Mardis and my copy editor, Dianne McBride for catching all my mistakes.

Thank you to my writing group friends: Maggie, Justin, Brian, Beverly, Carol, Rich, Barbara, Matt, Tim, and Sarah. Thank you to my critique group friends: Esther, Cathy, Bill, Susan, and Kelsey! You all have helped me grow as a writer over the last five year.

Thank you to my beta readers: Dianne, Stephanie, Verna, Lisa, Miriam, and Robin. Also thanks to my sister, Victoria, and her husband, Roy, for your input!

I am forever indebted to your generous sharing of knowledge and expertise, your critiques, input, and encouragement.

Thank you to my writing club students for being my   student   readers.

22689702R00075